Published by Yali Books, New York

Text copyright © Rukhsanna Guidroz 2018
Illustrations copyright © Debasmita Dasgupta 2018

Connect with us online -
www.yalibooks.com
Instagram / Twitter / Facebook (@YaliBooks)
Pinterest (@yali_books)

ISBN: 978-1-949528-99-2

MINA
VS. THE
MONSOON

RUKHSANNA GUIDROZ

ILLUSTRATED BY
DEBASMITA DASGUPTA

YALI BOOKS

Mina was
feeling sad.

4

She was watching peacocks walk past the mango tree outside her house, when one of them let out a piercing cry.

Mina knew the monsoon rains were coming. She was going to be stuck indoors all day.

AY-OOON AY-OOON

5

Mina peeked into the kitchen. "Can I play soccer?" she asked her *ammi*.

Her mother was humming a tune as she kneaded dough. "*Nahi beti,* stay inside. You will catch a cold in the rain. Let's celebrate the monsoon with *chai* and *samosas.*"

Mina crossed her arms.
"I promise I won't catch a
cold! I hate the monsoon.
I hate all the feasts and
songs. Scoring goals,
that's what I celebrate!"

8

KataKataKa**boommmm**

With a flash of lightning and a clap of thunder, it started to rain. The smell of damp earth filled the house.

9

Mina ran to her room. She took out a sandalwood elephant from her drawer and placed it on her blanket.

10

"Little elephant, Ammi doesn't understand. Running with the ball, weaving in and out until it's just you and the goal... she has never felt that explosion of happiness when you score!"

11

DIN DIN DIN DIN DIN DIN DIN DIN DAH DIN DIN DIN

Heavy rain drops drummed on the tin roof of Mina's house like a thousand fingers on a thousand *tablas*.

Playing the *tabla* always cheered her up. If she played loudly enough she might even chase those pesky clouds away. It was worth a try!

12

DIN DAH DAH DIN DIN DIN
DIN DIN
DIN DIN
DAH
DIN
DIN
DAH

Mina sat in her room and beat on the *tabla*. She played them until she was short of breath and her hands were sore.

It was time to check on the rain.

13

Mina looked out of the window. Her gaze was met by a sheet of silver raindrops.

Her heart sank.

From her window, Mina could make out a white smudge coming toward her house from the other side of the village. It was the *doodh wallah* on his bicycle loaded with milk cans.

15

"Does it have to rain?" Mina asked, as the *doodh wallah* handed her a jug of fresh milk.

16

"Yes, it does. Rice in paddies would die without water. And mangoes on trees would shrivel up. Mina, this is a time to dance and be happy."

Like Ammi, he too didn't understand. But his words made her think. Why not dance to STOP the rain?

17

Mina had everything she needed to dress up—bright gold *bindi*, red-orange *shalwar kameez*, copper-brown *henna*, and silver anklets. She admired her reflection.

A day without soccer? Never!

Mina went around in a circle, dancing to the beat of the rain. She tapped her foot here and twisted her wrist there. Her anklets jingled and her *shalwar kameez* swished. Sweat ran down her temples.

She was sure this had worked.

19

Mina groaned at the gray clouds still covering the sky.

"*Beti?*" Ammi came looking for her. "Still sad?" she asked, glancing at the soccer ball in her room.

Mina nodded.

"Stop sulking and fetch me some thread to string a flower garland. The clouds appeared today all of a sudden. Maybe like magic, they will disappear tomorrow."

Ammi had just given Mina a brilliant idea!

DIN DAH DIN DIN DAH DIN DIN DAH DIN

Mina faced her elephant and said, "Little elephant, I need your help with a magic trick. Let's make the clouds vanish so I can play soccer... today!"

DAH DIN DAH DIN DIN DAH

Mina waved her arms in the air to shoo the clouds away. She waited. Magic this big could take a while.

23

Mina remembered Ammi
had asked her for thread.
When she went to look for
it in her mother's cabinet,
Mina found something she
had never seen before.

She pulled it out and unfolded it.

It was a soccer jersey!

"It's mine." Ammi confessed. "I wore it when I was your age. Every rainy season, I would catch a cold. So I'd wait indoors, bored, until the sun came out."

"You played soccer?"

"Yes, just like you."

Mina slipped on the jersey.
A perfect fit!

28

It was time to see if her magic trick had worked.

The dark clouds were gone. The heavy rain had turned into a light drizzle.

"I did it!" Mina's eyes grew wide with excitement.

PLipPLip PLipPLip PLOP PLipPLip PLOP

In the pale light of evening, she saw a peacock
fly onto a branch. Another followed and
the pair sat sheltered from the rain.

Mina let out a joyous laugh. She now knew exactly what to do. "The two of us can play soccer, Ammi! If it rains again, we will hide like the peacocks so we won't catch a cold. We can celebrate with *chai, samosas*, AND soccer."

A slow smile spread across Ammi's face. "*Beti*, that's the best idea you have had all day!"

Out on the street, Ammi
passed the ball to Mina.

Mina kicked up a spray of chocolate-brown water and sent the ball...

...straight into the GOAL!

A helpful guide to the words in this book

(from the languages Urdu and Hindi)

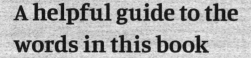

Mina (pronounced *mee-na*)

Ammi (pronounced *umm-mi)* - Mother

Nahi (pronounced *nah-hee*) - No

Beti (pronounced *bay-tee*) - Daughter

Tabla (pronounced *tub-lah)* - A percussion instrument with a pair of drums

Doodh wallah (pronounced *dhoodh va-la*) - Milk man

Bindi (pronounced *bin-dhee*) - A beauty motif, usually a small dot, placed between the eyebrows by girls and women

Shalwar kameez (pronounced *shall-var ka-meez*) - A traditional outfit consisting of a long tunic, a scarf and loose pants

Henna (pronounced *hen-naa*) - A plant dye used to create temporary tattoos on the palms and feet

A note for parents and educators

In villages like Mina's in the northern states of Bihar and Jharkhand in India, local organizations are trying to combat the common practice of child marriage by organizing soccer games for girls. Playing a sport provides these young women with a sense of accomplishment, helps them stay in school, and ultimately, challenges the idea that a girl's place in the world is at home.

For more resources, including an activity guide, visit our website and follow us on Pinterest (@yali_books).

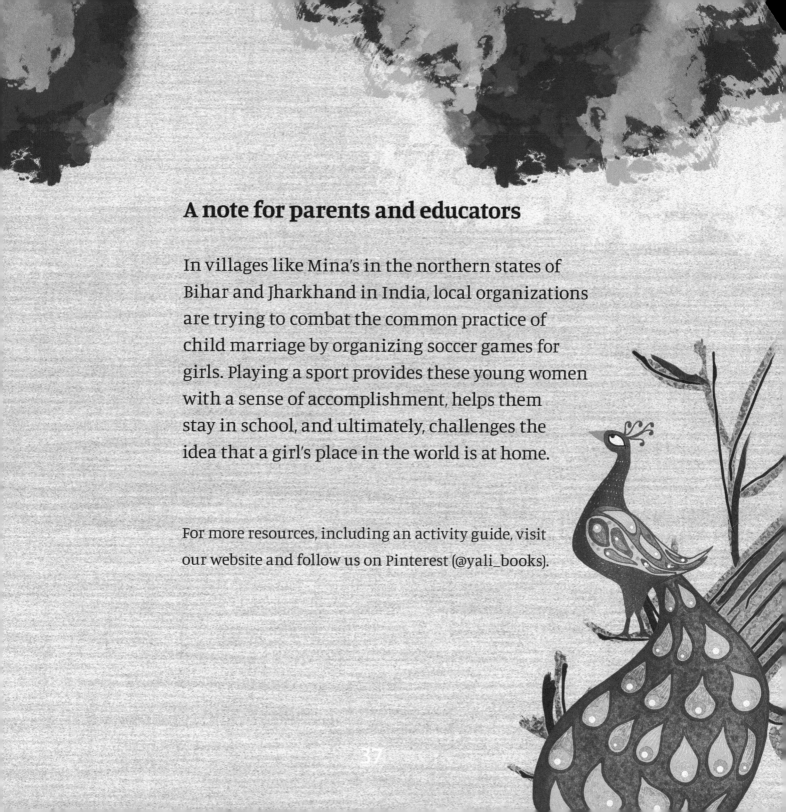

CPSIA information can be obtained
at www.ICGtesting.com
Printed in the USA
LVHW072037060619
620402LV00083B/38/P